Solo

Monologues for Drama

John Goodwin and Bill Taylor

Edward Arnold

© John Goodwin and Bill Taylor 1985

First published in Great Britain 1985
by Edward Arnold (Publishers) Ltd
41 Bedford Square
London WC2 3DQ

Edward Arnold (Australia) Pty Ltd
80 Waverley Road
Caulfield East
Victoria 3145
Australia

British Library Cataloguing in Publication Data

Goodwin, John, *1944-*
   Solo: monologues for drama.
   1. Drama – Study and teaching (Secondary)
   I. Title II. Taylor, Bill
   792'.07'12   PN1701

ISBN 0-7131-0955-6

All rights reserved. No part of this publication may be reproduced, stored in a retrieval system, or transmitted in any form or by any means, electronic, photocopying, recording, or otherwise, without the prior permission of Edward Arnold (Publishers) Ltd

The Authors would like to acknowledge the contribution made to the monologues by the pupils and ex-pupils of Dukeries School, Ollerton, Nottinghamshire.

Filmset in 12/14pt English Times by
Ceekay Typesetters Ltd, Sutton, Surrey

Printed in Great Britain at
The Camelot Press Ltd, Southampton

Introduction

Solo is a new form of Drama stimulus for the 14-16 age range. It can be used in a wide variety of subject areas and may be employed in the following ways:

1 As monologue speeches
Various examinations in Drama and English demand the presentation of a solo item. Apart from classical plays, it is often difficult to find material which suits the needs of the less academic pupil. The variety of *Solo* makes it possible to use the monologues with a mixed ability group. Many pieces – such as *Kaz, Thomo, Jackie, Hilary* and *Sam* – are quite short and use simple language, whilst others such as *Sarah, Charles, Muriel, Benjamin* make greater demands upon the individual and require a more subtle handling.

2 As a stimulus for individual and group role-playing
Many of the items included in this book have strong social themes and examine the teenager's relationship to adults, in particular parents, employers and teachers. After the pieces have been given to pupils to read, improvised dramas can be encouraged, using two or more characters.

3 As a starter for 'hot seating'
These items have proved valuable as a starting point for 'hot seating', a question and answer technique suitable for use in Drama, English, Social Studies, etc. The technique places particular emphasis on recreating and defining the lives of the various characters. Each pupil is given a few minutes to imagine charteristics of the *Solo* character he or she receives – e.g. name, description of personality, details of family history, etc. An individual is then placed in the centre of a circle (if available, a central spotlight in a dimmed room would assist atomsphere) and the rest of the group is encouraged to ask relevant questions. These questions are important to help pupils consider their characters' attitudes and motives. Questions may be of a general nature – e.g. 'what kind of person are you?', 'what are your interests in life?' – or they may concentrate on specific details taken from monologues, e.g. 'why does Kaz steal?', 'has Thomo always been in trouble at school?', 'does Jackie lie awake at night and think of Gary in hospital?'.

This can form an activity in its own right or lead to further exploration once the characters are more clearly defined in the minds of the participants.

4 *As a stimulus for group discussion and further script writing*
Having read the items, the pupils may wish to write their own monologues, relating the thoughts, feelings and emotions of their own characters. Likewise, the teacher may write his or her own solo items for use by group or individual.

5 *Teacher-in role*
It is possible to extend the range of *Solo* through a teacher-in-role method of teaching. In this way, rather than being an instructor outside the drama experience, the teacher participates in an active role within the drama experience. Any of the adult roles in *Solo* could accommodate such a strategy.

6 *As an extension of drama games and trust exercises*
Drama games and trust exercises are often the starting point for various areas of active lessons. It is possible to extend this activity through a thematic link with the monologues: e.g. games which involve stealing as a theme – (keeper of the keys, sly fox) could be further developed by referring to the shoplifting incidents involving Mr English and Kaz.

It is possible to use the *Solo* items purely as self-contained monologues but as indicated they can also be used as a stimulus for further Drama work. The appendix at the back of the book gives a more detailed guide for usage, providing specific instructions and suggestions as to how the pieces can be extended and explored.

J.G. and B.T.

Contents

1 School

see also: Leisure Louise; *Problems* Shane

Thomo	*suspended for fighting*	1	*51*
Thomo's Head Teacher		2	*51*
Colin	*the school bully/brag*	2	*52*
Pete	*a boy with a 'bad' reputation*	3	*52*
Mike	*a less 'well off' pupil*	4	*52*
Sonia	*talking about smoking*	4	*53*
Hilary	*a loner with a few friends*	5	*53*
Helen	*first day at school*	5	*54*
Roland Gee	*out of work school leaver*	6	*54*
Nadine	*awaiting exam results*	7	*54*
Andrew	*a school leaver remembering an old teacher*	8	*55*
Archie Connor	*school caretaker*	8	*55*

2 The Opposite Sex

Wendy	*receiving a Valentine card*	11	*56*
Jane Hawkins	*a girl's first date*	12	*56*
Oliver Perks	*a boy's first date*	13	*56*
Julie Walsh	*a pregnant teenager*	13	*57*
Mrs Walsh	*Julie's mother*	14	*57*
Will	*Julie's boy friend*	15	*57*

3 Leisure

Nicola	*a fruit machine addict*	17	*57*
Louise	*on punk hair fashions*	18	*58*
Lesley	*a fashion conscious teenager*	18	*58*
Jane	*on pop music*	19	*58*
Bernice	*on her Spanish holiday*	20	*59*
Sam	*on fishing*	21	*59*
Charlotte	*on eating out*	21	*60*
Danny	*on horror videos*	22	*60*
Beverley	*a football fanatic*	23	*61*
Lawrence	*her boyfriend*	23	*61*

4 Work

see also: Problems Annabel Mr. English; *School* Archie

Benjamin	an omelette fryer	25	*61*
Martin	involved in a youth training scheme	26	*62*
Tony	an apprentice starting work	27	*62*
Gordon	witnesses an accident at work	27	*62*
Jenny	a trainee hairdresser	28	*63*
Christine	a young mother and housewife	29	*63*
Muriel	early thirties, mother and housewife	30	*63*

5 Family

see also: Work Christine Muriel

Brian	who doesn't get on with his dad	31	*64*
Connie Spencer	mother of a handicapped child	32	*64*
Caroline	teenager getting home late	32	*65*
Graham Cowley	Caroline's father	33	*65*
Kath Cowley	Caroline's mother	34	*65*
Baby Ann	youngest of a family	34	*65*
Sarah	a girl with a sheltered upbringing	35	*65*
Liz	on her gran and old people	36	*66*
Joseph Brown	an adolescent who leaves home	37	*66*
Matthew Brown	his father	38	*66*

6 Problems

Charles	a disruptive boy, taken into care	39	*67*
Annabel	his social worker	40	*67*
Kaz	a shoplifter	41	*67*
Mr English	a store detective	41	*67*

Patrick	*a lonely boy in care*	42	*68*
Lucy Jackson	*remedial girl in care*	42	*68*
Kimberley	*a mentally ill adolescent*	43	*69*
Ruby Edwards	*a divorced alcoholic*	44	*69*
Jackie	*visiting her boyfried after a motorbike accident*	44	*70*
Jimmy	*a fan of James Dean*	45	*70*
Shane	*a vandal*	45	*70*

7 The Newcomer

Lynn	*a girl whose parents have split up*	47	*71*
Grandmother	*whom Lynn goes to stay with*	48	*71*
Ian	*the boy she meets*	48	*71*
Brenda	*Ian's ex-girl friend*	49	*71*
Carol	*Brenda's best friend*	49	*71*

8 Follow-up work   51

1 School

Thomo

(Thomo is fifteen and always in trouble. He has just been suspended from school for fighting.)

Watchit__! They call me Thomo. Me – I'm always in trouble. Can't resist a fight. I don't know why but I just see red. If somebody picks on me I have to fight back don't I? Why should they pick on me? Why should they pick on me just 'cause I'm small? When I had this skinhead cut they made me wear a hat just so no one would see me with it at school. Teachers, they're always pushing you about. Can't wait till I can leave school. See you.

2 School

Thomo's head teacher

I don't know what's happened. I've been a teacher now for eighteen years and there was a time when I used to enjoy my job. I used to feel I understood the children I taught, I could relax, have a joke, they'd tell me about themselves. But now it's all different. It's changed in the last five years, since I became a head teacher. The children look at me, they never say what they are thinking but I know what's in their minds. They think 'what does he know about me, silly old fool'. I try to bridge the gap between them and me but the gulf only widens.

Take Craig Thomson for instance. He's waiting outside my office now for fighting. He's the tenth boy I've seen this week about causing trouble in school. I shall have to suspend him – I have no choice, even though I know he's not a bad lad at heart. I shall have to play the part of the strict head teacher. But wouldn't it be a change for me to say, 'Thomo, here, have a cigarette!' But I can't do that. After all, I'm a head teacher!

Colin

(Colin is a boy of about 14. He likes to think of himself as a bully. Brags a lot.)

It's tough here. You got to watch yourself. Things happen. There was this kid once – Justin. Right little weed, snivelling, right wimp. When he started moaning, you wanted to thump him, real hard, really beat him up. He was like that. Got on our nerves. No one liked him.

Not me. No one. Even teachers didn't care for him. So one day we decided we'd had enough of friend Justin. We decided his number was up. So we done him.

It wasn't just me. Whole bunch of us. We all planned it.

That lunch break, we went off down the bike sheds when no one was looking. He had this grotty little blue Raleigh. Remember it well. Didn't take much doing – we cut the brake wire. Even an idiot could've seen it. We gave him his chance.

Then that evening after school he goes bombing down the hill like he always did. Only he couldn't stop, could he? Gets to the T-junction and – splat! Straight under a Ford Escort.

It's like that this place. You got to be able to look after yourself. You got to be careful. You got to be liked.

Pete

(Pete is a teenager who comes from a family with a 'bad' reputation at school.)

Teachers, they never give you a chance. First day at school and they start. 'Name?' Peter Wallis. And that's what does it. As soon as they hear the name Wallis they think of my brother Robert. They sneer and say 'I hope you're not going to turn out like your brother, always in trouble, I'll have to keep an eye on you'. Next thing you know they start calling me Robert, get me mixed up with my brother.

Robert left last year. Well, he had to, they expelled him. And now if there's any trouble in class they blame it on me, even though I've done nothing. It's always been like that – he has the fun and I get the blame.

4 School

Mike

(Mike, a boy in his early teens, talks about pocket money.)

Some kids get £5 pocket money a week, videos for Christmas, music centres for birthdays. Others get taken off to Majorca in the middle of winter. Jock Wilson, for instance, he went there right in the middle of exams, missed the whole lot. To make it worse, he came back really brown – here we had rain for two weeks.

We had to do a survey in maths the other day. A survey on pocket money. We found out that out of 30 of us, more than 20 got over £2 a week. When the teacher asked me how much I got I couldn't tell the truth. I just lied. I don't get any, you see. I used to, but not now. Not since my dad left.

Sonia

(Sonia is a clever girl who rarely gets into trouble at school.)

Did you know, more girls under 17 smoke than boys? They reckon it makes them slimmer. Most of my friends smoke. They meet behind the chemistry labs at break. I'm sure the teachers know they're there but no one bothers about it. They all turn up late for lessons stinking of stale tobacco.

My dad smokes, so does my mum. But I don't. The odd one out you might say. If only they could see the colour of their lungs. I lie awake at nights listening to my dad coughing away. Cancer's not the only thing smoking brings – there's bronchitis, pneumonia, heart disease and lord knows what else. I've nagged my parents to give up. I wish they would. But no, they say they haven't the willpower.

Why don't people have the courage to give up?

Hilary

(Hilary is a teenager who finds it difficult to make friends.)

I dread subjects where you have to get into small groups – PE, Drama, sometimes English. I dread it because I get left out. No one will have me in their group. I'll be by myself – alone. I'll have to tell the teacher I haven't got a group. He'll make a fuss and put me in one. Then when his back's turned they'll pick on me, tell me I stink, tell me they hate me. Why do they hate me? Why don't they want me in their group? Why?

Helen

(Helen is 8 years old and talks about her first day at school.)

Mum brought me to school and I was very scared and the teacher said hello and all the other children looked at me and one girl began to laugh, I don't like her. Mum said she would come for me at lunchtime and I wanted to cry but I didn't because that girl was looking at me. The teacher made me sit down and she gave me all these books and a pen. I blotted over my first page. The sums are too hard, I've never done these before. I bet Mary and Jane are having craft lessons now. Mary and Jane were my best friends.

The bell went and I didn't know what to do and the teacher said did I want to go out to play. The girl sitting next to me said 'come on, you can play french elastic.' I went outside and the girl who laughed at me was there. When it was my turn she pulled the elastic and I fell down and cut my knee. I didn't cry. The teacher put a plaster on and some magic cream, she said. Then we had singing and that girl kept sticking her tongue out at me and at last it was lunchtime and my mum came and I cried all the way home.

Ronald Gee

(Ronald is aged 16 and can't get a job anywhere. He worked hard at school, didn't get into any trouble, but still can't get a job.)

Ronald is the name, Ronald Gee. I'm sixteen – sixteen and no job. I've tried everything and everywhere and they just don't want to know. Come back next week, sorry no vacancies or just simply ignore you – won't answer the door. Do you know, I've written off for 78 jobs and not even had an interview.

Yet I left school with 5 O-levels. You know what they tell you at school – get your nose down, work hard, behave well and you'll get a good job when you leave.

Where are all the jobs?
Where are they?
I wish someone would give *me* a job.

Nadine

(Nadine has recently finished school and is waiting for her exam results to arrive. It is early morning and the post has just been delivered.)

They've still not arrived! They should have been here by now. Maybe second post. I don't think I can wait much longer. I suppose I could phone the school, but I don't want to hear my results over the telephone, I want to see them in black and white.

What am I going to do if I don't get the grades? That last History paper was terrible – I know I've failed it. I know I have. None of the right questions came up. We were told that Henry VII's foreign policy was a dead cert this year. I spent three whole days on that alone, but it didn't come up after all. And English was a disaster too – I didn't even understand the question on 'Macbeth'. I'm sure it's all gone wrong. I felt quite confident two months ago but now, the longer I wait the worse it all seems.

Three months of revision, sleepless nights, getting ill, sitting exams, working my mind into a frenzy, and now everything depends upon a small sheet of computer printout. Why doesn't it arrive?

Andrew

(Andrew has recently left school and during the time he is looking for a job he spends some afternoons in a large park.)

It's quiet here in the park. You can walk right round the lake on some days and never see anyone. Watch the ducks, give them bits of bread, just sit and think. Sit on this park bench. It's got a plaque carved on it. It says 'In memory of George A. Wilkins.' Who's George A. Wilkins, you ask? You've never heard of him? Well I'll tell you. He was my old teacher at junior school. I can see his face now. I was nine and a very quiet pupil. One day Mr Wilkins brought in a bowl of daffodils. 'Children,' he says, 'these daffodils will open tomorrow and we shall be able to admire their beauty.' I don't know what made me, but that night when all the class had gone and Mr Wilkins was not in sight I crept back to the classroom. I tore off all those daffodil buds. After I'd done it I opened my hand to look at the crumpled remains of the buds. No one ever did find out who'd done it. Nobody suspected me. I didn't own up. Mr Wilkins died last year, it was in the newspapers. So I sit on this park bench and say, even if it's too late, 'Sorry Mr Wilkins . . . sorry Mr Wilkins.'

Archie Connor

(Archie is in his late fifties. He is a school caretaker.)

Kids! What am I going to do about them kids? Where's the sense in it? During the day wild horses couldn't drag them into school but at night – well, the night's different. They all turn up, whole gangs of them, rushing round all over the place, skidding their bikes across my playing fields. Takes me hours to get the fields right.

They reckon they're just having a bit of fun. Fun! Smashing windows, wilful damage to public property. I can't have kids coming in here breaking windows – makes me look like I'm not doing my job properly.

Now don't get me wrong, I can take a joke. No one can say Archie Connor can't take a joke. Only, after a while it gets a bit much. After a while I get a bit fed up of these kids, coming in here, making my life a misery. I mean, looking's one thing, vandalism's another.

2 The Opposite Sex

Wendy

(Wendy is a retiring girl of 13 who has not yet been out with a boy. It is Valentine's Day and she has just received a card.)

A Valentine card. For me? It must be, it's got my name on the envelope. No one's ever sent me one before. Who would send *me* a Valentine card? And not just any Valentine card, but one with a red silk padded heart. And stamped across it in gold letters 'To my darling'. And inside, a verse:

> A rose's perfume fades away
> The sun goes down at close of day
> The lark's sweet song's so briefly heard
> And 'I love you' but three short words
> Yet while sweet nature's fruits subside
> The strongest love will never die.

Who can it be from? Michael Challender? It hasn't got a name at the end of the verse, just a question mark. Yet I'm sure it's Michael Challender. It must be Michael Challender. I've always loved Michael Challender with his blond curly hair and his big blue eyes. It *must* be him.

Only it's not his handwriting. I know only one boy who crosses his t's like that. Piggy Reid. Piggy Reid sent me this as a joke, just to make a fool of me.

Still I don't care. It's the thought that counts. And I think it's from Michael Challender.

Jane Hawkins

(Jane is 13 and has just been on her first date with Oliver Perks.)

With my blusher and my 'Charlie' I thought I could hardly fail. The hours I spent in front of the mirror! I was determined to look my best. We'd arranged to meet under the bank clock at seven. I got there at quarter past. My friend Sandra said you should always be late for your first date, and she's been on plenty of dates, has Sandra. She'd warned me about what could happen and boy was she right! It was just like on the telly. There he was in his tight denim jeans. Cool as you like he said, 'Let's go for a walk'. We went down the park. He was so experienced. He knew just how to kiss. I'd read about it in *Oh Boy* but I never thought it would happen to me. I shall never forget my first date with Oliver Perks.

Oliver Perks

(Oliver is 13, wears glasses and has skin trouble.)

I'd never have the nerve to ask a girl for a date. When it was arranged for me to go out with Jane Hawkins I began to panic. I didn't even know if I wanted to go out with her. After all, I didn't have anything decent to wear, just a pair of flared trousers. I felt a fool. No one has flared trousers these days. We arranged to meet under the bank clock at seven but the bus was late and I got lost. It was after half past by the time I got there. I felt so flustered when I saw her that I began to stutter. Then she started shouting at me and asking me where I'd been and that just made my stutter worse. At last I managed to say 'where shall we go?' She didn't have any ideas either. We decided to walk to the bus station. Should I hold her hand? I asked myself. But try as I could I didn't have the guts to do it. Then she turned to me and asked me if I wanted to kiss her. I didn't know what to do. I don't know what made me but I just ran off. Oliver Perks, you'll never forget your first date with Jane Hawkins.

Julie Walsh

(Julie is an intelligent girl in her last year at school, who finds she is pregnant.)

Pregnant. Yes, I'm pregnant. I'm going to be an unmarried mother at sixteen. My parents don't know. I can just hear my mother's voice – 'Five minutes of pleasure for a lifetime of misery, young lady, that's what you can expect.' But it doesn't have to be like that. And the father? It's Will. He says he wants to marry me. I think he even loves me. But I won't marry him. I'm not sure, you see, not sure I love him, not sure I should trap him into a marriage we'll both regret. There's always the other way – abortion. But I've thought it over and I've decided to keep the baby and give it my love, my care, my life.

Mrs Walsh

(Julie's Mother)

Julie's been so quiet lately. I know something's worrying her. We used to be able to talk about everything. We were always very honest with each other, but now it's different. I've asked her what's wrong but she says, 'It's nothing mum, don't worry.' But I do worry. She's behaving so strangely, she acts as though she's scared of me. Why should she be scared?

    I hardly dare admit it to myself but I think she's pregnant. If she is, she'll need all the help she can get from me, because she'll certainly get none from her father. . . . Julie, I know what you're going through, because the same thing happened to me. I had hoped you wouldn't make the same mistake as I did but if it has happened, well . . . Julie, please tell me.

Will

(Will is a teenager who is to be the father of Julie's baby.)

It's one of the proudest moments in anyone's life when you know you're going to be a father. It proves you're a man. When Julie told me of course I was shocked but as I love her it didn't seem to matter too much. Then she said she wouldn't marry me. She wouldn't say why at first, just burst into tears. Then after a while she said she didn't love me. I was lost to know what to say. Love? Love? She doesn't know the meaning of the word 'love'. Well I reckon it's the end of us, of Julie and me. Seems so sad really.

3 Leisure

Nicola

(Nicola is 17 years old and addicted to playing fruit machines.)

I could give up any time I choose, I'm not an addict. People tell me I am but I'm not. It's just – well – when I see a fruit machine I can't help myself. There's something about the spinning wheels, the clatter of tokens. Playing fruit machines is . . . magical.

    I once won eight pounds. I put it all back in, of course. That's the only problem, it's hard to stop once you've got into the swing. And it costs so much. Sometimes I spend all day in the arcade. Last week, it cost me £20, nearly all my wages. It doesn't bother me as long as I don't think about it. And it's not as though I've got anything else to spend the money on. I don't know many people so there's nowhere to go really. Except the arcade. And it's my money, so why all the fuss?

Louise

(Louise likes to dress in punk gear and is in her last year at school.)

What's wrong with dyed hair? Come on, tell me, what's wrong with it? My boyfriend Des and me decided to have matching colours. I had orange with blue stripes and he had blue with orange stripes. Next thing I knew we both had to go and see the headmaster. 'Is this a conspiracy?' he says. 'The staff are refusing to teach you. You are both a visual distraction to the rest of the pupils.' I wondered what he was going on about, 'visual distraction'. What's he mean? Well, we got sent home and told not to come back until our hair was back to its normal colour. Great, I thought, a holiday from school. After a while though it got boring with nothing to do. My mother says I've got to have my hair back to normal by tomorrow. But Des and I decided we'd have a laugh – we're both going to have mohicans.

Lesley

(Lesley is a fashion-conscious teenager at a party.)

Oh my God, look at her, oooo er! Where did she get that gear from? And look at her hair! Had her mother's curlers in all night I'll bet. Why doesn't she get it cut and dyed? She's got that lousy old skirt on as well. That's the fourth time she's worn that to club. I'd be ashamed to wear it. It only cost £5 you know – probably got it from a jumble or

Oxfam shop or something. I reckon she wears her mother's clothes you know. Fancy wearing that pink top with that modern romantics skirt!

You know she fancies Ted. Christ she's got a hope of him looking at her! Oh no, she's got a pair of high heels on. They're lousy. Ha! Ha! She can't do that dance with those shoes on. I don't want her coming near me. Somebody might think she's with me. God I hate her!

Let's beat her up at school tomorrow, hey?

Jane

(A teenager's view of pop music.)

I had this boyfriend – he was dead keen on music. You should've seen his stereo, and all his records. I listened to them every Sunday afternoon, sitting on the floor in his mum and dad's dining room, rock music blaring out. We used to like opening the window because he had this old cow as a neighbour. Playing records at full blast, especially ones with any swearing on. Steve's dad said he'd break the rude records if he found out which ones they were. It was really great that summer.

Anyway, we finished, but my mum and dad bought me a record player so I've got hold of a few records. I never buy that slushy stuff – that's crap! I like music with a message to it. Something loud and angry. Most of my mates at school don't like it, but there's a couple of us the same, so we like to stick together.

I got some headphones recently. It's great. I can listen to my stuff as loud as I like – even the swearing ones – and no one bothers me. Your ears ring for days after you've had headphones on. You can't hear what teachers say!

Bernice

(Bernice, a teenager, comments on her recent holiday in Spain.)

We just been to Spain. It was crap.

I didn't want to go in the first place but I didn't get a choice. I wasn't asked or anything, just carted off with me mum and dad and our Neville. I told them it would be crap but they didn't listen. They had to find out for themselves!

The hotel was all in one piece but that's about all you could say for it. Food was awful – half cooked, half cold. Only good thing about the grub was that there weren't much of it. They were dead stingy.

At night you couldn't sleep because of the disco. Me dad wouldn't let me go to the disco. I didn't want to go anyway. I wasn't having my bum felt by some greasy bullfighter.

And that's another thing – the bull fights. We didn't go to that either. Me dad again, he stopped us. He's like that – anything that sounds exciting he's dead against. I didn't want to go anyway. Who wants to watch a bull getting slaughtered and pay for the privilege? No ta.

There's really nothing to remember about Spain. Most days we just walked round the shops, and spent the evening in the hotel bar. It was too hot to go sunbathing. I didn't want to anyway. I hate sunbathing.

We only went a week. Felt like a month. £600 down the drain, that's what I think. Dad says next year we're going to Blackpool. Not that I want to really. I hate Blackpool.

Sam

(Sam is fourteen and spends every spare minute he has going fishing.)

I could spend all my time fishing. I'm here today for twelve hours – eight o'clock this morning until eight tonight. Don't I get bored? No, not me. Time just seems to fly. When I'm fishing the time passes more quickly than when I'm doing anything else. Not like school – there I'm forever looking at my watch and minutes seem like hours. Here I can relax, see patterns in the water, hear the call of birds, enjoy the fresh air. Your mind goes blank and you forget nagging parents, homework and kid sisters. You just keep your eyes on the float, waiting for it to plunge and then you know when it does that you're in for fun. Fishing, I love it!

Charlotte

(Charlotte is fourteen and has just been out for a meal with her parents.)

Last night mum and dad took me out for a meal. We went to this really posh restaurant where it costs you £5 to have a glass of water. There was this bloke in uniform, like an out-of-work soldier, to collect our coats. I didn't want to take mine off but mum insisted. I've never felt so daft. Then we went into this huge dining room. Dad had reserved us a table. I don't know why because we were the only ones in the place. There were staff, bar maids, waiters, managers and god knows who else just standing round the edge of the room staring at us. And all those knives and forks! Where do you begin? I didn't know a soup spoon was different from a pudding spoon, trust me! And the food! It was just a nightmare. I felt sick and just wanted it to end. I kept wondering why we were the only ones there. Then I got a closer look at the manager. He was just like Dracula! Oh no, perhaps we were trapped in Dracula's castle! Give me fish and chips anyday!

Danny

(Danny is 12 years old and likes to watch horror videos.)

You seen *The Dead Alive*? It's brill. That bit where the zombie's hand comes through the window and strangles the old dear, and her face goes purple and blood shoots out of her ears! It was better than that *Trial of Terror*, that was rubbish. It had a few scary bits but there wasn't much blood. It's the blood I want to see. Like in *Dracula Awakes* where you see the stake driven into his heart and all the blood spurts into that bloke's face.

I used to watch all those before my mum stopped me. She got a letter from school saying horror videos were bad for us and we shouldn't watch them. But I don't see the harm. It's not real life, is it? Just a good laugh really. Now I'm only allowed to hire Walt Disney or kids' stories. They're boring. I don't see why I shouldn't watch horror videos if I like them.

Beverley

(Beverley is a teenager and an ardent follower of football.)

God, you should've seen the goal I scored! Brilliant. Julie sent a long pass out of defence and I picked it up on the halfway line. There was three of them between me and the goal. I dummied the first two and put the ball under the legs of the third. Then the goalie came off her line and I just lobbed the ball over her head. One–nil! Nothing beats the thrill of football.

People say I'm crazy but I'm not. I like other things. My boyfriend Lawrence, for instance, riding on his motorbike, going to the pictures. But when I'm out there, on the terraces or with the football at my feet, then I really come alive. It's another world.

Lawrence

(Lawrence is a teenager with no interest in sport. His girlfriend Beverley is football mad.)

I ask you, a girl mad on football! It's not natural. Football's a man's game. It's OK for lads to leap up and down on the terraces if that's what they want to do, but girls! That's different. But take Beverley, my girlfriend, she spends every spare minute she's got following football. She gets *Shoot* every week, never misses 'Match of the Day', goes to see United when they're at home, and worse than that, she even plays. Yeh that's right, she plays! They've got their own all-girls team and their own league and everything. Whenever I go out with Beverley all she talks about is who won the cup in 1956. I mean, there's a place for everything. God, I hate football.

4 Work

Benjamin

(Benjamin is 17 and has been out of school for a year. He works in a restaurant, frying omelettes.)

I'm what you call a specialist. I specialise. I got this job, see – chef's assistant. I fry omelettes. My speciality.

It's funny how you get lumbered. I'd just left school, wasn't doing much, kicking me heels – then there was this ad in the paper. Holiday camp. They were looking for all sorts. That's where I started frying. Worked in this take-away they had, frying fish. And chicken. Same thing really, just came out of different boxes. I did that for the summer, then when the season ended I moved down here. I thought the change would be a good thing.

I got a job in this little Italian restaurant. They wanted someone to do the omelettes. I learnt the whole range –cheese and onion, ham and mushroom, Spanish. Spanish omelettes are my best. You got to get the blend right see – chop up your veggies, beat your eggs 'til they're just so, always keep a constant heat. Everything's got to be exact. It's an art really, it's a knack.

I don't mind frying omelettes. Gets a bit boring sometimes but it's good to have something you're good at. It's nice to have a speciality.

Martin

(Martin is sixteen and has been involved in a youth training scheme.)

Rip-off! That's all it is – a rip-off. They fixed me up with a training scheme working with this electrician. I had an interview. 'One day a week off to go to college, proper training, good lunch breaks', they told me. Then I started. 'Sorry we can't give you the day off,' they said. We had twenty minutes for lunch if we were lucky. We started at 7.30 in the morning and carried on until 7 at night. Twenty-five quid, twenty-five lousy quid. After stoppages, board for my mum, I'm left with five pounds. Five quid to last a week. I want to pack it in, it's no better than slavery, but my dad won't let me. He says, 'You're lucky to have a job or be on a scheme whilst there's millions on the dole. Perhaps there'll be a permanent job at the end of it.' But this electrician bloke, he treats me like dirt. What should I do?

Tony

(Tony has just started an apprenticeship in an engineering works.)

It's a laugh really. They're a friendly lot here. So long as you can take a joke and give a joke, you're in. Take my first day. Jim – that's the charge hand – says, 'Go to the stores young lad and ask for a long weight.' I goes to stores and the big fellow there, bald as a coot, says, 'What you come for?' I says, 'I've come for a long weight.' Half an hour passes and there I am still waiting. Baldy comes back. 'Excuse me,' I says, 'but what about my long weight?' Without even a smile he says, 'You've just had it.' It was only then that I saw the joke. Mind you, I got my own back. Next day I put laxative powder in the charge hand's tea. I've never seen anyone run to the gents as quick as he did. Work? It's just one big laugh.

Gordon

(Gordon is 17 and has been working down a mine since leaving school.)

The first thing they tell you when you go down the pit is never take risks. 'Think safe and you'll be safe,' they say. They told us that on the surface, and the sinking feeling in my stomach as I went down in the cage brought home how dangerous the pit can be. But as the days and weeks pass you forget the fear. I did. Until that day.

I'd been told to work with Harry Boyd. We were on the

coal face. When you change the cutter you're supposed to turn off the power. But Harry didn't bother, it was too much trouble he said. After all, he'd changed the cutter that way for the last five years. The cutter takes minutes to cut through a coal seam but it only took a fraction of a second to sever his leg. It wasn't a pretty sight. I shall remember the look on his face for the rest of my life.

Jenny

(Jenny is 17, a trainee hairdresser.)

When I left school I had a couple of CSEs, nothing much but it was just enough. I'd always fancied the idea of being a hairdresser. You meet all kinds of people, and it's not just like any other job. It takes a lot of skill.

I work at this place called 'Gerard's'. To begin with all I did was sweep up and make coffee. But once a week I go into the tech on a course and they teach us everything about cutting hair and styling and all that.

Sometimes if they're rushed in the shop, I get to do some shampooing, and soon I'll be able to start practising properly. At the moment I'm only let loose on dummies. I did my friend Bridget's hair last week though, and she was really pleased with it.

When I'm qualified I want to start up my own hairdressers, working on my own, going to people's houses. I like the idea of being my own boss, and if I'm successful and make some money, I might even take other people on to help me. I wouldn't boss them about though. I don't see why people should be bossed about, do you?

Christine

(Christine is 18, married, a mother of two.)

Everyone said it wouldn't last. 'You shouldn't rush into things,' my parents said. But I'd been going with Simon for two years so it was hardly a hasty decision. Most of my friends thought I was pregnant – why else get married at 16, they thought. It never occurred to them that I might *want* to get married, that I *wanted* to settle down with Simon. After all, he had a steady job, we'd found a nice little flat – getting married seemed the obvious thing to do. Why wait?

The twins were born a year later – Sophy and Deborah. They can be quite a handful, everything has to be done twice: two mouths to feed, two nappies to change, two sets of milk teeth! But it's a matter of organisation mainly. It gets you down sometimes of course, when the kids are bawling and the cleaning has to be done. But being a housewife and mother is a better job than the ones most of my friends have. They come round on their days off and moan about the shop or the factory. Then they tell me I ought to be depressed or bored being stuck at home, never going out at nights. But it's not like that, not for me at least. I enjoy my life, it's a new experience.

Muriel

(Muriel is in her early thirties. She has been married since leaving school and has three children.)

Women's liberation has certainly done nothing to help me! When you've got three children and a husband to look after, there isn't much time to think about anything else, what with all the usual daily chores. Rodney, my husband, says I should get out more, but he still expects to find his tea ready when he gets home. And lord knows what the kids would do if they got back from school one day and found the house empty. A woman's place is in the home!

I used to enjoy running a family. I used to feel needed. But now I feel used instead. If I tell Rodney how I feel he'll accuse me of watching feminist programmes on afternoon telly. In his book, feminism is just an excuse for women to moan. His idea of equality is drying the dishes.

There's no escape for women like me, is there?

5 Family

Brian

(Brian is a teenager who doesn't get on with his father.)

Me and me dad, we don't get on. Mutual. Never have. Don't know why. There's something there that's all – when I look at him there's something I don't like.

Know what he does? Sits in an art gallery all day. Sits on a plastic chair and watches people go by. All day, five days a week. Reads his newspaper, spends his money on the horses. Never goes anywhere. Never takes me anywhere. Never does anything.

That's not living, not really. He just watches other people's lives, that's all he does. Wouldn't think you could feel anything for someone like that. I do. I hate him.

Connie Spencer

(Connie Spencer is in her late thirties and has two teenage daughters, Emma and Rachael. Emma is a mentally handicapped girl.)

You hear so much these days about teenagers always falling out with their parents. This hasn't happened with my two. We're closer now than at any time I can remember. Why? Because of Emma. You see, Emma can't do much to look after herself because she's mentally handicapped. Rachael does everything for her, dresses her, teaches her how to do things, looks after her. You'd think Rachael would get fed up with it but she doesn't. She doesn't seem to want many other friends and as for boys, well she's not interested. And if anyone is cruel to Emma, calling her names and that, Rachael is there to sort it out. When the doctor first told me Emma would never be able to live a normal life I was horror-struck. I wondered if I could ever care for her or look after her. I thought – some people would moan if they got a blister on their toe and here am I with all this trouble. But isn't it funny, out of that trouble has grown our closeness, our love.

Caroline

(Caroline is 16. She arrives home late from a disco and is about to go into the house.)

Is that the time? Is it really quarter to twelve? Oh dear, the lights are still on. They're waiting for me. I don't think I can face a scene now, I'm too tired. I just want to go to bed and sleep. But no, we'll be up for another half hour screaming at each other. Dad'll want to belt me and mum will look all hurt, and we'll all end up saying stupid things that we'll regret in the morning.

Maybe I should have let them know I was going to Greg's for coffee. Trouble is, if I'd told them they'd never have let me go. They treat me like a kid who has to be watched over and locked up for her own safety. It's all so silly and petty. Surely it's time they learned to trust me!

Graham Cowley

(Caroline's father. He is waiting for her to arrive home.)

Where is she? I won't have a daughter of mine out at this time of the night. She's only sixteen. When I was sixteen we had to be in by nine thirty and it's now a quarter to twelve. It's happened before. Last time she said she'd been to the youth club. Youth club! That closes at nine thirty and in she strolls at 11 o'clock. That youth club is five minutes down the road – a dead dog could crawl the distance in ten minutes, but it takes her an hour and a half.

But she's never been this late before. Where is she?

Kath Cowley

(Caroline's mother. These are her thoughts as she waits for her daughter to get home and listens to her husband Graham ranting.)

Can't he stop for a moment? Doesn't he know how nervous it makes me, watching him pacing up and down? The more angry he gets, the worse it makes me feel. Where is Caroline? I'm sure she's had an accident, I'm sure something dreadful has happened. Why don't I do something? Why am I sitting here watching Graham turning purple? I ought to 'phone the police or go out and look for her. He'd only say I'm being foolish, wouldn't he?

And yet . . . I know she's been late before, but she's never been out past half eleven. Caroline, I wish you'd come home.

Baby Ann

(Ann is 14 years old and is the youngest child in her family.)

I used to love being the youngest. I've got a brother and a sister, they're much older than me so I used to get away with all sorts of things. Whenever we played games they let me win. When my brother started work he bought me sweets and records, anything I wanted. And my sister let me practise wearing her make up. Dad said they spoilt me rotten. I suppose they did.

Trouble is, you never stop being the youngest. I still get

called Baby Ann. I'm fourteen years old! I didn't used to mind but now, well, I don't like being treated like that any more. Last year my brother gave me a new doll for Christmas and he couldn't understand why I wasn't pleased. I can't be Baby Ann all my life. Why won't they let me grow up?

Sarah

(Sarah is in her teens. She has lived a very sheltered life, free from cares or troubles.)

I don't know why it happened. Is there ever a reason? We were so safe, so happy. I used to curl up in bed at nights and feel so secure, just lying there listening to the murmur of voices from downstairs.

I remember a warm summer's night. We had spent the day at the beach, the whole family – mum, dad, my brother Tommy and me. It was a gorgeous evening so we had supper in the garden. Dad cooked hamburgers on the barbecue and we sprawled ourselves across the lawn and just lay there. I remember the smells – the mown grass, the scent of the flowers. We ate the hamburgers with pickles and cheese and crisps. Then when we'd finished, Tommy told us some of his silly jokes, and we all laughed. They weren't very funny, we'd heard them before, but oh how we laughed!

We laughed a lot in those days.

But of course we didn't know that it wasn't going to last. It never even occurred to us.

Until one day I got home from school and heard someone crying upstairs. For the first time in my life I felt afraid. I crept upstairs and stopped outside my parents' bedroom. I listened to my mother crying. I stood by the door and listened to the harsh lonely sobs. And it was all gone. The laughter. The summer evenings. It was all gone.

Liz

(A teenager's view of old people.)

Some old folk are OK, but some are always moaning. Me gran, she's great. I'm her only grandchild, you see, so I get what I want. She likes to sit and talk. It's a bit of a bore at times but I don't mind really 'cause she makes great cakes, especially vanilla slices. She listens too. I tell her everything and she's got time, not like me mam who's always busy. I like me gran but I think she gets lonely.

I don't like all old folk though. There's them that push you in shops. They think 'cause you're a kid and they're old it gives them a right to get served first. Why should they? They've got all day, they've got nothing else to do. Then there's them that's always moaning at you 'cause you're scruffy and noisy or 'cause you've chased their cat or walked on their wall. Bet they did the same when they were kids but they just have to spoil everything. It's a crime to have a laugh. Grumpy old sods. Me gran's not like that – well not with me anyway. She lets me stay up and watch telly till me mam and dad come in.

Joseph Brown

(Joseph has recently dropped out of sixth form at school and 'escaped' to a remote area of Scotland.)

I feel . . . it's like . . . don't know – confusing, so confusing, you know? Like I don't know who I am. Like seeing a stranger in the mirror. Sort of unreal.

Never used to think about what I wanted. Never seemed to have time. Everything was sort of fixed, planned, kind of definite. Work, school, exams. Never had time to think, just had to keep on working, keep on grinding away. It was so . . . really so bizarre. My dad, he used to lock my room. Meant so much to him I suppose. He'd never done anything, he wanted me to do all the things he'd never done himself. He thought that was maybe possible.

And me – I just, I suppose I just wanted him to like me. Worked hard, played along. Just wanted him to like me. Just didn't want to be hated.

Yeh but you reach a point . . . sort of, can't go on. Feel sort of tired, sort of, drained, wiped out. Don't feel real anymore. Don't feel right. You have to, sort of, get away. Go away somewhere. Far away. Just try and find out what you want. What you *want*. What *you* want.

Matthew Brown

(Matthew Brown is a man in his late forties. His son Joseph has just dropped out of the sixth form and left home.)

I did everything for Joseph. I worked seven days a week, twelve hours a day sometimes. Sent him to the best school my money could buy. I didn't want him to end up driving lorries like me. He was a bright kid, no doubt about that, true potential, someone to be proud of. He could've done anything – gone to college, got a degree, taken up a profession, anything. He just needed the push.

I haven't seen him for two months. Last I heard he was living in some kind of commune in Scotland. A son of mine!

It hurts. All that encouragement, all that support and guidance, all that money, all those sacrifices – what is there to show for it? A kid with eight O-levels living like a peasant.

As far as I'm concerned, he doesn't exist anymore.

6 Problems

Charles

(Charles has a record of disruptive and 'anti-social' behaviour. At 15, he has been taken into care by the local authority.)

What are you staring at? Do I offend you or something? Get in your way, do I? Upset you? Yeh, well that's tough, isn't it. I'm here now. I'm your responsibility now. I'm your problem now.

    I didn't ask to come here, you know. And no one asked me either. No one said 'Look Charles old chap, do you mind awfully, we'd like to take you away and examine your brain.' I didn't get a say. Nothing new in that. By the way, do I have to stay here? Do I have a choice? No, thought not.

    Where's Annabel? I'd like to 'phone my social worker. If I'm going to be carted off against my will she should at least be here. She's supposed to be looking after me. Then again, if she knew how to do her job properly, I wouldn't be here in the first place, would I?

Yeh, this is all her fault. And the old dear's. The old man too. They're all to blame. It's a plot. They're probably all in it together. I would blame myself but of course I can't be held responsible, can I?

Annabel

(Annabel is a woman in her late twenties/early thirties. A social worker.)

Sometimes I wonder if it's worth the effort. As though I don't have enough problems of my own without taking on everyone else's.

Charles has been in and out of trouble since the day he was born. A natural rebel. He's difficult to understand. He expects me to be able to help him, but he can't seem to help himself.

His latest problem is stealing. We could all see it coming, all of us – parents, teachers, even Charles himself – we all knew how it would end. There's an awful kind of inevitability about it all. Trouble at home. Trouble at school. Trouble with the police. An almost logical sequence – from the cradle to the reform school.

It's difficult to find a place for Charles. At fifteen, society has already rejected him. And unfortunately, he's bright enough to realise that. What hope can I give someone like that?

Kaz

(Kaz is a teenager who spends little time in school.)

Do you know why I nick stuff? I do it for kicks. I always feel a thrill when I walk out of a shop and know I've got away with it. It started off with my mates as a dare. 'I bet you daren't Kaz'. I dared, I did. It started off with chocolate bars. Now it's anything. I fancy it, I grab it. I know what you're thinking – you're thinking what'll happen to me, where will it lead to? I don't think of that, I just nick.

Mr. English

(Mr English is in his sixties and has worked as a store detective in a large department store for several years.)

I hate my job, can't wait 'til I retire. I dream of getting my feet up, stretched out on the settee, watching television. Do you know why I hate it? I'll tell you – kids. Kids, nicking stuff. Year in, year out, day in day out it gets worse. It's so pointless. Take yesterday – girl comes in here, truanting from school. Looks around in a sneaking way, didn't see me watching her. When I caught her she had two cheesegraters, a flan case, a packet of marbles and a packet of walnut whips stuffed up her jumper. I caught her red-handed and all she could say was 'I don't know how they got there.' It isn't as if she needed any of the stuff. It's so pointless.

Patrick

(Patrick is in his early teens and lives in a home for problem children. He is a very nervous slow-speaking character. He has few friends.)

I don't like it down where I am.
 You don't know what it's like. I mean . . . they look after you I suppose. Food's all right I suppose. Get a bit of money sometimes. Sometimes, go out places, out in the country, in the old van like . . .
 Mrs Daws, she's all right sometimes. Talks to me sometimes, when she puts the lights out, sometimes kisses me, on the cheek, like. But she ain't always there. Sometimes it's one of the others – they just lark about. They don't care.
 And Mr Hardy, when he's about, wants to know all what we're up to – where we've been going, when we'll get back, that sort of thing. Have to be in by ten. Trouble else.
 I don't feel good. Down there.
 You don't know what it's like.

Lucy Jackson

(Lucy is thirteen and lives in a children's home. She has a mental age of seven.)

Hello, my name's Lucy, Lucy Jackson and I'm five years old. My mummy and daddy left me when I was . . . two. That's why I'm here at Greenfield's Children's Home in Sidcup which is in Kent. I want to live with Aunty Jean and Uncle Frank. Uncle Frank left and Aunty Jean didn't want me any more.

Aunty Ida comes and visits me sometimes but lately she hasn't been. She says she's busy but I know that she doesn't love me.

Why doesn't she love me?
Why does no one love me?
Why does no one love me?

Kimberley

(Kimberley is 18 and lives in a mental hospital. She sits clutching a doll.)

Mad? . . . I'm not mad . . . who says I'm . . . My baby . . . my baby . . . *(she sings)* 'Where are you going to my pretty one, I'm going a –' . . . Round and round the garden like a teddy bear – round and round and round and round . . . this little piggy went to market, this little piggy stayed at home and this little piggy *(she shouts)* had a baby . . . Don't take my baby away . . . *(She produces a carving knife and stabs the doll)* This little baby must die, die, die, DIE!

(She looks up.)

Why do you stare at me? Don't stare. I can see your eyes, all your eyes and they stare. Don't stare. Please don't stare. No, no, no, no, no . . .

Ruby Edwards

(Ruby is 35. Her husband David has just left her and she has turned to drink for some comfort.)

Just another drink, just one more, just a little one, why not? Won't do any harm. It's no use, you can't forget. You've drowned your sorrows in gin till it comes out of your ears. You remember the pain, the tears, the anguish you felt when he left you.

Try counting sheep – one, two, three, four, five *(louder)* six, seven eight . . . It's no use . . . try something else, think of a new dress, a meal out, snowdrops in Spring.

'A meal out' – who'd take me out for a meal? Bad breath, face so ugly –

David would – David . . .

Just another drink, just one more, won't do any harm.

Jackie

(Jackie is 18 and is visiting her boy friend Gary in hospital. Gary has had a motorbike accident.)

Gary . . . Gary . . . I know you can't hear me Gary but all I want to say is . . .sorry. If we hadn't had that row and you hadn't ridden off as angry as you were . . . I know it's all my fault that you are lying here . . . a cabbage . . . perhaps never to know anything again. Never know a kiss, never see a snowdrop in Spring, never know how I love you, never . . . Just one sharp bend, a patch of ice and then blackness, a living death. Of course the doctors tell you different, say there's still hope, but I know different. Gary I know we shall never be together again. Goodbye Gary.

Jimmy

(Jimmy is about fifteen. He is a small boy, wears glasses and has his hair greased back.)

Don't you think I look like James Dean? I'm a dead ringer for James Dean. It's the eyes that does it. We got the same eyes. Me and James Dean – we could've been brothers.
   I've seen all his films – *Giant*, *East of Eden*, all them. It's uncanny, seeing him up there like that. Sometimes, I watch him on the screen and it's like I'm looking in a mirror. Spitting image.
   He's dead now of course. James Dean, dead and buried now. That's the difference, I suppose. He died young, like heroes do. And that's the difference. James Dean is immortal and me – I'm just . . . alive.

Shane

(Shane is 15 and enjoys vandalising property.)

There's only one crime – getting caught. That's the only thing that gets you into trouble. Me, I make sure I don't get caught. Work on your own, that's the secret, see. Don't have people hanging round. And don't go for the obvious. I never touch 'phone boxes – everyone does 'phone boxes so there's more risk getting caught.

I do trees mostly, and windows. Council put these rows of little trees down the bottom of the shopping centre. Right pansy looking, they are. Dead easy to shift, just have to bend them back and they snap in two. I've done those trees loads of times. Have to keep going back, you see, because the council keep replacing them.

It's just like that with the windows up the school. Sort of a game really. No matter how many I smash, they all get replaced and I have to go back and do them again. I'm not complaining though. I like a challenge. One night, I did a whole row of windows, must have been eight or nine. Then the old caretaker got wise and I had to scarper. He reckons he'll get me one day. No chance!

It's a laugh, doing the school. If I had the chance – if someone said to me, we want you to demolish the whole school, that'd be like a dream come true. I'd kick and smash everything in sight, 'til there was just a heap of rubble. That's what I like doing, see. I like destroying things. That's all I ever want to do.

7 The Newcomer

Lynn

(Lynn is 15. Her parents have split up and she has been sent away to stay with her grandmother. She stands at the door of her grandmother's house, about to ring the doorbell.)

This isn't going to work out. I bet she's not even expecting me. Or if she is expecting me, I bet she doesn't want me here. After all, she's my grandmother and there's such an age difference between us. She'll probably treat me like a baby, and she'll go on about the war and how much prices have risen. I'll have to sit quietly, only speak when I'm spoken to and all the time I'll be wishing I wasn't there. I'll be wishing my mum and dad hadn't split up. I'll be wondering why they did. When I press this doorbell and my grandmother comes to the door it'll be a new start. But I don't want a new start. Why can't things be like they were?

Grandmother

(Lynn's grandmother stands at the window waiting for her granddaughter to arrive.)

She said in her letter she'd be here at five. Now, have I got everything ready? The bed's aired, tea's prepared. Did I remember to get some barley water? Yes, I did. It's been such a long time since there were any young people in the house. It'll be nice to have company. But it is eight years since I've seen her. She'll have changed since then. What shall I say to her? I must try not to go on about the old days, she won't want to hear about that. That's not what a teenager is interested in.

Ah, someone's coming down the path. That can't be Lynn. She looks so much older, so grown up. It must be her, though – who else could it be? I feel all in a spin. Well, I'd better answer the door. I hope we're going to get on.

Ian

(Ian is the same age as Lynn. They meet while she is staying with her grandmother.)

I think I'm in love. Yes, I know I've said that before – seven times in the last three weeks to be precise – but this time I mean it. She's not like the girls round here. They're OK I suppose if you want a laugh. But Lynn's different – I don't know how, but she is. She doesn't know anybody here. She's only here because her parents have split up.

She didn't say much about it and I can't help feeling she's very upset and unhappy. It's up to me to make her feel as though she's welcome, and help her get to know people.

But what about Brenda? What am I going to say to Brenda? You know how stroppy she gets . . . Oh, I can't be bothered with Brenda now. All I care about is Lynn.

Brenda

(Brenda is Ian's ex-girlfriend. She is at a disco.)

Well look who's just come through the door. If it isn't loverboy himself and there's whatsherface, the thing he's been seen with. They've got a nerve coming here. I wouldn't have minded being ditched for someone decent but her – god, look at her! What can he possibly see in that? They walk in here as though they own the place, so sure of themselves, all smiles. They won't be smiling by the time I've finished.

Carol

(Carol is Brenda's closest friend.)

The trouble with Brenda is that she never knows when to stop. She's gone too far this time. I've always been her mate in the past, I never held anything against her, even when she took my Warren off me, but now I can see what a bitch she really is. It's not as though she cared for Ian –

after all, she was seeing lots of other lads apart from him. She did it out of jealousy, she wanted to get her own back. She just wanted to show off in front of everybody and look big. She thought she was being really clever but she's done it now. Brenda's all right if she's the centre of everything. But I'm fed up of getting into trouble because of her. Next time something like this happens she'll be banned from the disco. That's not going to happen to me. Now's the time to find a new friend. That new girl, Lynn, she seems all right. Maybe I'll get to know her.

8 Follow-up work

Thomo *Page 1*

Thomo's head teacher *Page 2*

1. *For discussion*
   a) Why has Thomo been in trouble at school?
   b) How do you imagine Thomo's home background? Does he have brothers or sisters? Is the family a single-parent family?
   c) What could be the more positive sides to Thomo's character? Is he fond of animals? Does he have a girlfriend?
2. *Pair or group work*
   In pairs, or groups, discuss the characters further.
   Using the monologues as core material, act out the following scenes:
   a) Thomo's suspension interview in the Head's office –how do they interact? Bring out the main parts of each character.
   b) Thomo talking to his mates after the suspension interview.
   c) Thomo at home after being suspended.
   d) Thomo's parents' visit to the school.
   e) A scene depicting Thomo ten years later.
   The class may all act out the same situation or different groups can choose different ones which they can then show to each other.
3. Write or improvise a small scene on the subject of authority.

Follow-up Work

Colin _Page 2_

1. *For discussion*
   How far do you think Colin is telling the truth?
2. Act out the following, using the monologues as a core:
   a) Colin with his mates before and after the boasted incident
   b) Colin meeting a younger boy at night in the school yard.
3. Write or improvise a scene on the subject of boasting. You could try these:
   a sporting feat
   an act of bravado
   a con trick
   a boast which relates to school.

Pete _Page 3_

1. Two people, one playing a teacher, the other a pupil, should act out the following (if possible, try to make as few people aware of what you are about to do):
   The teacher on duty around the school confuses the pupil with a different pupil, and imagines that this pupil has done something against the rules – smoking, breaking school rules, fighting, etc. –although he or she might be entirely innocent. Act this situation out to the rest of the class without too much initial explanation.
   Discuss this short scene in relation to the monologue.
2. Work on the following scenes:
   a) Pete with a teacher with whom he has a good relationship
   b) Pete and Robert at home
   c) a scene in which mistaken identity leads to a false accusation.
3. Write or tape a scene on the theme of prejudice.

Mike _Page 4_

1. Try this game. Three envelopes marked A, B and C are placed in a space in front of the class. Three volunteers participate in the game, each of which throws a dice. The person with the lowest score takes envelope A – inside is a note 'no pocket money, single parent family'. The person with the second lowest score takes envelope B – inside is the note '£1 a week'. The person with the highest score takes envelope C – a note inside says '£5 a week, Dad is a company director'.
   Mike is the person who picks up envelope A. Act out what follows.

2. Act out the following using the monologue as a core:
   a) the day Mike's dad left
   b) the day Jock returned from holiday
   c) window shopping.
3. *For discussion*
   a) How can Mike help himself to a happier life?
   b) Will Mike resort to crime in order to make up for the financial hardship which he feels?
4. Write or perform a scene on equality.

Sonia *Page 4*

1. Split up into groups of four or five and make a still picture or tableau of some scenes based on:
   a) a gang with someone trying a cigarette for the first time
   b) the secret gang of smokers behind the bike shed at school
   c) an operation – the surgeon operating for removal of a cancer caused by smoking.
   Ask other members of your group to give these tableaux titles and then bring them to life, acting out each scene.
2. Using the same groups, make up an advert with a suitable slogan or jingle to show the dangers of smoking.
2. Using the monologue as a core, act out the following:
   a) the pupils tempt Sonia to start smoking
   b) Sonia persuades her parents to give up smoking.
3. *For discussion*
   Which of your group smokes? Are there any reasons why you should give up smoking?

Hilary *Page 5*

1. Try this game:
   Make a circle by linking hands or arms. One person must try to get into the circle as it moves around. 'Get out' or 'Go away' or some such chant can be yelled if considered appropriate.
2. In small groups, perhaps pairs, act out scenes in which Hilary meets the other characters from this section – Thomo, Mike, Andrew, etc. Through role play explore how she interacts with these characters. Does she find she has something in common with any of them?
3. Write a story on the theme of isolation.

Follow-up Work

Helen
Page 5

1. On your own, using the monologue as a core, think about Helen's character – her personality, parents, background etc.
2. Try this hot-seating activity:
   Choose one person to play Helen. Other members of the group ask her questions about 'herself', e.g.
   – 'What did you fear most about your first day at school?'
   – 'What did you enjoy most about your first day at school?'
   – 'Did you find a teacher you liked?'
   – 'If you are eight, what previous school did you attend?'
   – 'Can you tell us about your second day at school?'
   In this way, try to find out as much as possible about Helen.
3. Act out Helen's last day at school.
4. *For discussion*
   Did you share Helen's fears on your first day at school?

Ronald Gee
Page 6

1. Set up mock job interviews. Teachers and careers teachers might be willing to help.
   See if you can get some help with how to act at an interview, and what replies to give.
2. Act out the scene where Ronald revisits his school, using the monologue as a core.
3. *For discussion*
   Youth unemployment.

Nadine
Page 7

1. Using the monologue as a core, act out the following scenes:
   a) the night before a big exam
   b) Nadine receiving her exam results – this can be a solo performance.
2. *Game*
   Make a chart with the following information on it:
   – the names of people in your group
   – imaginary exams they have sat
   – imaginary results
   Act out your response to these results.
3. *For discussion*
   Discuss the merits of the exam system. Are exams necessary? What does the system tell us about the society in which we live?

Andrew

1. Act out the morning after the daffodil incident. The person who plays Andrew does not have to deny the incident as in the monologue. The teacher in role as Mr Wilkins asks 'Do you know anything about the daffodil?'. The rest of the class form a 'path of decision'. This is best seen in diagrammatic form:

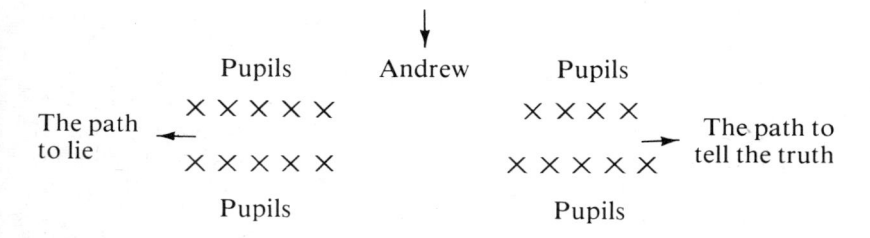

```
                        ↓
            Pupils    Andrew    Pupils
The path   × × × × ×           × × × ×     The path to
to lie   ←                              →  tell the truth
           × × × × ×           × × × × ×
            Pupils             Pupils
```

The pupils who sit on the path give the thoughts in Andrew's mind as he comes to a decision. Those on the path to lie might say:
- The truth will hurt
- Only a little white lie
- He'll never know

Those on the path to truth might say:
- It's always best to tell the truth
- Come on Andrew, own up

Andrew will decide upon which voices are the most persuasive and turn down that path.

2. Try also the following scenes based on the monologue:
   i) a scene in Mr Wilkins' classroom
   ii) Andrew destroying the flowers
3. Write or tape a scene on guilt.

Archie Connor

1. Imagine what it's like doing Archie's job. Do you think he is a sympathetic character? What do you think he is like at home? Try acting out scenes showing aspects.
2. You can also link this monologue to Shane (page 45) and imagine a scene where Archie catches him.
3. Write a script on the generation gap.

56 Follow-up Work

Wendy *Page 11*

1. As an introductory activity, design a joke Valentine card.
2. *For discussion*
   Do you think Michael Challender sent the Valentine? Try to work out what Wendy looks like. Find adjectives to describe her appearance.
3. *Role-play*
   On your own act out Michael Challender receiving a card from Wendy.
4. Write or perform a scene on loneliness.
5. Try this idea.
   Work in pairs. Nominate an 'A' and a 'B'. 'A' takes the role of Wendy, 'B' is one of Wendy's class mates, who has heard a rumour that Wendy has received a Valentine Card. Act out the scene between them. Does Wendy tell the truth?

Jane Hawkins *Page 12*

Oliver Perks *Page 13*

1. *For discussion*
   a) What is the worst thing about a first date?
   b) Why do Jane's account of the first date and that given by Oliver differ so much?
   c) Which version is nearer to the truth?
2. Write down what happened in your last Drama lesson and the one before that – if you can remember! Do this either individually or in pairs. Compare your accounts with others.
3. *Role-play*
   (i) Imagine yourself to be either Jane or Oliver and try to build up a picture of the character. Choose a volunteer from the group and place them in the centre of a circle and ask them questions about their character.
   (ii) In pairs act out one of these scenes:
   a) Sandra chatting up Oliver
   b) Jane trying to borrow her older sister's make-up
   c) Oliver's best friend discovering details of the date.

Julie Walsh	*Page 13*
Mrs Walsh	*Page 14*
Will	*Page 15*

1. *For discussion*
   Should Julie keep the baby? Do you think it is the end of Julie and Will's relationship? What should Mrs Walsh say to Julie?
2. *Role-play*
   In pairs and or threes act out the following:
   a) Mrs Walsh confronting Will
   b) a meeting between the three characters
   c) Julie and Will together after the birth of the baby.
3. Tape or write a scene in which a girl deliberately gets herself pregnant.
4. Sooner or later Julie will have to break the news to her mother that she is pregnant. Act out this scene or other scenes when breaking news is concerned, e.g. a death, failing exams, moving house.

Nicola	*Page 17*

1. As a group, discuss the monologue and the character of Nicola. Possible questions that might be raised:
   a) is Nicola really an addict?
   b) how serious is her addiction?
   c) what kind of advice or help could she be given?
2. *Pair work*
   Nominate an 'A' and 'B'. 'A' takes the role of Nicola, 'B' acts as her conscience or 'inner voice', and has the task of trying to persuade Nicola to stop gambling.
   Alternatively, act out this process in a scene between Nicola and her best friend.
3. *Group work*
   Set up an 'addiction clinic'. Select 3 or 4 members to role-play addicts (e.g. drug, alcohol, work, TV) and improvise a scene in a waiting room. The rest to the group observe their behaviour and try to determine what kind of treatment they might be given.
4. In smaller sub-groups work with an 'addict' individually in a counselling session. This might be further developed through role play with key scenes showing the progress of treatment.

Follow-up Work

Louise   *Page 18*

1. *For discussion*
   Should pupils be sent home from school because they have dyed hair? Should boys be sent home if they have a skinhead haircut or very long hair?
2. Try this activity. Divide into groups of 4 or 5. Two of the groups give as many reasons as possible why pupils should be sent home in these circumstances. Three of the groups find as many possible reasons why the pupils should not be sent home. The arguments can then be presented directly or in role, e.g. a group of teachers meet in school and present the arguments, or a group of pupils or parents present a petition in support of, or opposed to, dyed hair.
3. *Role-play*
   Try these scenes:
   a) the scene between Louise or Des and the head teacher
   b) Louise comments on her own daughter's hair and fashions 15 years on
   c) your own scene or story showing the influence of a cult or the media, e.g. clothes, fashion, pop music.

Lesley   *Page 18*

1. *For discussion*
   Why is Lesley so jealous? Will Lesley attempt to beat up the girl in school the following day?
2. *Solo work*
   Describe what Lesley is wearing. Write down a list or prepare it as a monologue. You could do this as if you were the girl Lesley is describing.
3. *Role-play*
   a) In pairs, improvise a scene between Louise (see previous monologue) and Lesley.
   b) Act out the party scene as a whole class play. Let the focus of conversation switch from one group to the next. Try your own scene or story on the theme of jealousy.

Jane   *Page 19*

1. Imagine Jane forms a rock group. Act out these scenes in the story of the group:
   a) the first rehearsal
   b) a split in the group

c) interest by a manager
d) the first gig – the possiblility of a double booking and another group arriving to play.

You don't have to be able to play instruments in order to do these scenes.

2. *For discussion*
Take different styles of pop music and different groups. Prepare short talks on their contribution to the pop scene.
3. In the monologue Jane says that she likes to play records at full blast. Act out a scene when she has a record full blast and her Mum or Dad return home after a hard day's work. Does the scene always have to result in conflict?

Bernice   *Page 20*

1. Write a few lines for an imaginary holiday brochure advertising the attractions of your home town. Exaggerate its 'selling points' as much as you can without actually lying!
    As a whole group, read out the accounts and consider to what extent they distort reality. How would you feel as a visitor arriving in the town on the recommendations of the brochure?
2. Having read the monologue 'Bernice', discuss the character and her general attitude to foreigners and holidays. In building the character, it might help to think about her tone of voice and manner of speech.
3. In small groups, inprovise a scene showing the family's reaction to Bernice's unenthusiastic behavour. Possible settings for the scene:
    a) in the hotel bar
    b) arriving home from the holiday
    c) getting ready to go on holiday.
4. As a contrast to Bernice, write your own monologue for the character 'Neville'. Imagine that he thought Spain was great and really enjoyed the holiday.

Sam   *Page 21*

1. Sit by yourself for a few minutes and try to remember times in your life when you have been in a world of your own. This could even be when you have been surrounded by a crowd of people, but, in your imagination, alone. Times like – when you're reading a book, taking part in sports, listening to records. Describe to other members of the class what you felt like and where you were.

60 Follow-up Work

2. *Pair work*
   a) Imagine you are fishermen. Tell each other stories about the one that got away or other far-fetched incidents.
   b) Using the same idea, change the characters from fishermen to others, e.g. two race horse owners describing their proudest moments.
3. Still in pairs, imagine Sam is fishing without a licence and in private water. Along comes a water bailiff. What happens? Can Sam talk his way out of the situation?

Charlotte *Page 21*

1. Try to imaging the meal out from the point of view of Charlotte's Dad or Mum. Create your own monologue.
2. Act out:
   a) A scene in a restaurant where an ordinary person is confused with a famous person. (e.g. someone who looks just like a rock star). The 'celebrity' is given a free meal and the best service, only to be revealed as a case of mistaken identity, at the end of the meal.
   b) A different night out with a teenager and parents.
3. *For discussion*
   Why does Charlotte hate the meal so much? Might there be reasons which she does not explain?

Danny *Page 22*

1. In small groups of 4 or 5 make a still picture tableau of a poster advertising a new horror film. You might wish to title the 'film' yourselves or ask other members of the class to think of an appropriate title.
   As a whole group, pick out one still picture that you feel would make the most horrific/frightening film.
2. Read the monologue 'Danny'. Decide whether or not you agree that horror films are harmless.
3. *The Debate*
   As a whole group, create a setting (e.g. village hall, censor's office) where the debate will take place. Appoint a chairperson (possibly teacher-in-role) and other roles you feel relevant, e.g. film director, film censor, local cinema owner, local councillor, worried parent, etc.
   Enact through improvisation a meeting to decide whether or not a new horror film (perhaps the one chosen from 1.) should be

shown to the public. The debate can take various forms and should be organised by the chairperson who is responsible for the order of speakers.

At the end of the debate, take a vote of the whole group to decide whether or not the film should be released to the public.

Beverley *Page 23*

Lawrence *Page 23*

1. *For discussion*
   Why is Lawrence so opposed to football? Is it football he really dislikes or the fact that Beverley is involved in it?
   Can you imagine any other situations which girls would normally be expected not to be involved in?
2. Act out:
   a) *in large groups* a tribe or civilisation in outer space where women are considered superior to men. Into this situation enters a man from Earth or England.
   b) *in small groups* The day the girls' team wins the league.
   c) *in pairs* an argument between Lawrence and Beverley.
3. Write your own story about sexism.

Benjamin *Page 25*

1. Think of a hobby or interest that you have and prepare a one-minute talk on the subject that you might give to the whole class. Alternatively, you may choose to explain your specialised interest to just one or two other members of the group.
2. In small groups, develop a piece of improvised drama centred around the character of Benjamin. Suggested scenes:
   a) Benjamin at work
   b) Benjamin a few years earlier, opting for cookery classes at school
   c) Benjamin facing redundancy.
3. As a whole group, set up an improvised situation entitled *The Reunion*. The setting is 10 or 20 years in the future and you have returned to the school for a reunion.
   Imagine either what you think you'd be doing in the future or alternatively what you ideally hope to be doing. Think about what sort of 'specialities' you might have acquired.
   You might also choose to consider how you feel you might have changed personally.

Find out what other members of the group have become – what are their jobs? How have they changed? Have you anything in common with them?

Martin   *Page 26*

1. *For discussion*
   a) Would you advise Martin to continue with the scheme, or to give it up and sign on the dole?
   b) How else could Martin sort out his problems?
   c) Do you think the monologue portrays a realistic picture?
2. *Role-play (in pairs)*
   a) Martin in dispute with his boss as he asks for better conditions.
   b) Martin with his dad.
3. Write or tape a play, or story, about exploitation.

Tony   *Page 27*

1. Scenes to act out:
   a) after Tony has been at work for some time he tries a trick of his own on a new apprentice.
   b) a practical joke which goes wrong.
   c) the day Tony was made redundant.
2. To think about:
   Why is work so important to people?
3. Create your own monologue about someone who loses their job.
4. Think about Tony's character. Is he the kind of person you would like to have as a friend? Why is he always cheerful? Imagine his trick on the charge hand becomes the talk of the works. By using several groups talking at teabreak, show how the incident becomes exaggerated and changed as people retell the story.

Gordon   *Page 27*

1. To think about:
   Is a miner one of the most dangerous jobs you can have? List in order of priority ten really dangerous jobs. What makes these jobs dangerous? Could any of these jobs be done by machines, without the human element? If this is possible would it be a good idea?
2. *Role-play*
   a) breaking the news to Harry Boyd's family
   b) an accident at work

Follow-up Work

c) a person in a secure and steady job decides to abandon it to become a racing driver or to take a very dangerous job. Show the reaction of friends and family.

3. *A final activity*
   Make a list of safety guidelines for people working in coal mines.

Jenny — Page 28

1. As a group, discuss what each member thinks they'll do after leaving school.
   It might also be relevant to discuss any work experience that members of the group have had, and possibly also their experience/opinion of careers advice in schools.
2. Think about the character of Jenny. What is her attitude to work? Are her plans for the future likely to materialise?
3. Develop a piece of drama dealing with one of the following situations:
   a) Jenny losing her job at 'Gerard's' due to a cutback in trainee staff.
   b) Jenny in the future as boss of her own business, employing a trainee hairdresser.
   c) a day in the life of 'Gerard's' hairdressers.
   d) a group of ex-schoolfriends, meeting and discussing their differing experiences of life since leaving school.

Christine — Page 29

Muriel — Page 30

1. Compare the two characters, either through group discussion or by a process of role play and hot seat questioning.
   Consider how their attitudes differ on such subjects as:
   a) women as 'housewives'
   b) teenage marriage
   c) feminism
   d) raising children.
2. In small groups develop a piece of drama showing Christine's relationship with her husband, Simon. You might choose to consider what their marriage will be like 10 years on.
3. In small groups develop a piece of drama concerning Muriel's relationship with Rodney.
   Alternatively, role play a scene showing what happens when Muriel announces she is going 'on strike', or joining a women's movement.

64 Follow-up Work

4. Choose a setting where Christine and Muriel might meet (e.g. launderette, supermarket, playgroup). As a starting point, imagine that Muriel has recently joined a feminist group and is trying to persuade Christine to come to one of their meetings.
   This piece of drama could be developed by the whole group with several other scenes showing how women's rights relate to or conflict with the traditional concept of family-mother-wife.

Brian   *Page 31*

1. As a whole group, sit in a large circle. Nominate a 'leader', who then names an adjective relating to mood or attitude. Introduce yourself to other group members adopting the mood given by the leader. Continue until the leader shouts out another adjective. Possible adjectives: 'sad', 'excited', 'shy', 'aggressive', 'confident', intense', 'callous', 'polite'.
2. Read the monologue.
   Discuss Brian's attitude towards his father – why does he hate him? Is his attitude justified?
   Consider also what kind of character Brian's father is, and what his attitude towards his son might be.
3. *Pair work*
   In pairs role play a scene between Brian and his father (e.g. at home having a meal together).
4. Consider other parent–child relationships and improvise a scene contrasting the one between Brian and his father.

Connie Spencer   *Page 32*

1. *For discussion*
   a) Why does Rachel seem to care so much for Emma?
   b) Will Rachael always be so close to Emma?
      Can you imagine circumstances when she would not be prepared to look after her?
   c) Can you imagine a situation when Emma could help Rachael?
2. Act out the following:
   a) the doctor telling Connie that Emma is not a normal baby
   b) a character other than Connie coping or attempting to cope with disability
   c) a scene between Rachael and Emma
   d) a character who is the girls' brother enters the situation and strikes an unsympathetic attitude.

Follow-up Work 65

3. *A final point*
   How do *you* respond to mentally handicapped people when you meet them?

Caroline Cowley	*Page 32*
Kath Cowley	*Page 34*
Graham Cowley	*Page 33*

1. *For discussion*
   Can you remember times when you have been late home? Were there occasions when it caused your parents real worry? Were there instances when you believe your parents behaved unreasonably? Why do parents sometimes lose their tempers at these times when at other times they stay cool?
2. Act out:
   a) Caroline's arrival home
   b) Caroline's arrival home the following night.
3. Write or tape a story or play on the theme of parental authority.

Baby Ann *Page 34*

1. As a group, discuss some of the following points:
   a) why won't Ann's brother let her grow up?
   b) how do you think Ann behaves at home?
   c) how do you think Ann behaves at school and/or with friends?
   d) what can Ann do to make her family accept that she is no longer a child?
2. Develop through improvisation one or more of the following scenes:
   a) Ann taking her new boyfriend home to meet the family
   b) Ann at 16/17, announcing that she is leaving home
   c) Ann with friends, meeting her brother in the street.

Sarah *Page 35*

1. Choose one member of the group to read the monologue and role play the character of Sarah. A spotlight in surrounding darkness might help create the right kind of mood for this piece.
   As a group, ask 'Sarah' about her family background and the sudden change in the home situation. The nature of the questioning should take account of the character's mood – avoid interrogation techniques.
2. Follow-up scenes for small group inprovisation will depend upon the information 'Sarah' gives the group. Discuss how the family's

life has altered and develop a piece of drama showing how they cope with the new situation.
3. Other scenes could be developed on:
   a) how Sarah's mother copes with life as a single parent
   b) someone facing up to a new role involving responsibility.

Liz   *Page 36*

1. *For discussion*
   a) How do you feel about Liz's comment 'some old folk are O.K.'?
   b) Why do you think Liz seems to like her Gran so much?
2. Act out:
   a) Liz visits her Gran
   b) A crisis in Gran's life in old age.
   c) Gran looks back to her youth. Act and narrate.
3. Write or tape a story called Gran's entry into the old people's home.
4. *A final point*
   How would you feel if you were old and had to enter an old people's home?

Joseph Brown   *Page 37*

Matthew Brown   *Page 38*

1. Select two members of the group to play the characters of Joseph and Matthew. By hot seat questioning, build up a picture of their relationship by examining the past events between the two.
2. If the role-players consent, you might also observe the re-enactment of certain scenes from their past, e.g. Matthew confronting Joseph over a disappointing school report; Joseph asking his father if he can go out to a party.
3. Consider the character of Joseph's mother. What kind of relationship would she have with her son e.g. sympathetic, indifferent, overbearing, etc.?
4. In small groups, improvise one of the following scenes:
   a) Joseph at the 'commune' in Scotland
   b) Joseph being visited by his father and/or mother
   c) Matthew meeting the son of a work colleague. The boy used to be a close friend of Joseph's and is now doing well at college.
   d) Joseph 20 years on, perhaps with a son of his own.

Charles	*Page 39*
Annabel	*Page 40*

1. Two members of the group are selected to read the monologues and role play the characters.
    i) 'Charles' reads his monologue to the group. By a process of hot seat questioning the group find out more about his background and personality. Some pertinent questions might be:
        a) why are you in care? What have you done?
        b) who is Annabel?
        c) what is your home like?
        d) why are you 'not responsible' for what happens to you?
    ii) This same process is repeated with 'Annabel' in the hot seat. Questions about her job and the role of a social worker might help build a picture of the character, as well as more specific questions about her relationship with 'Charles'.
    iii) The two players are asked to re-create the last meeting between Charles and Annabel prior to Charles going into care. The scene is observed by the group.
2. *Discussion*
    Discuss the observed scene and consider what other scenes could be acted out to examine the characters further. It might be relevant by this stage to place particular emphasis on what will happen to Charles in the future.
3. In small groups improvise one or more of the scenes or events discussed.

Kaz	*Page 41*
Mr English	*Page 41*

1. Try this game, called 'Keeper of the Keys'. Its theme is stealing.
    The class sits on the floor with each person in a space of their own. One person is blindfolded and placed in a space a little apart from the rest of the class. He or she sits cross-legged with a bunch of keys within arm's length upon the floor, holding two rolled up newspapers. The object of the game is for one of the class members, one at a time, to 'steal' the bunch of keys away from the blind-folded keeper of the keys and return back to their place without being touched by the newspaper. The blind-folded keeper can attempt to swat at the stealers at will but must not move from their cross-legged position.

68 Follow-up Work

2. *For discussion*
   Why does Kaz steal? Are there reasons other than that she does it 'for kicks'?
3. Act out the following scenes:
   a) Mr English catching Kaz shoplifting
   b) Kaz in court
   c) Kaz with her parents.
4. Write out or tape a different scene or story about shoplifting.

Patrick   *Page 42*

1. *Solo work*
   Sit or lie in a space away from the rest of the group. Imagine that you are totally alone, isolated. It might help to recall a past experience of being alone. Think about how you felt at that time – were you lonely, bored, content? Quietly speak your thoughts and feelings aloud to yourself.
2. *Pair work*
   Role play two characters meeting by chance late at night. Both have just run away from home but for different reasons: 'A' has left home through boredom and is looking for some kind of adventure; 'B' feels rejected and wants to find somewhere to belong. Improvise how the two characters react to each other.
3. Select two group members to role play the characters of Mrs Daws and Mr Hardy as mentioned in the monologue. By a process of hot seat questioning ask these characters in turn to tell you about Patrick. If their accounts differ strikingly, discuss why this might be.
4. Further scenes that might be acted out:
   a) Patrick's first day at the home
   b) Patrick with Mr Hardy after getting home late
   c) Patrick with other kids from the home
   d) Mrs Daws and Mr Hardy deciding what to do with Patrick following a mischievous 'incident' involving the boy.

Lucy Jackson   *Page 42*

1. *For discussion*
   Why does Lucy have a mental age of seven?
   Why do you think her parents placed her in the home?
   Can you imagine what her parents were like?
   Do you think it's true that no one loves Lucy?
2. Act out the following scenes:
   a) Lucy's parents' decision to place her in the home
   b) the visit of Aunty Ida
   c) a new friend for Lucy

Follow-up Work   69

    d) your own scene about someone shut away from the world – prison, hospital, etc.
3. Write your own story about someone else who feels no one loves them.

Kimberley   *Page 43*

1. *For discussion*
   Is Kimberley insane? Who does she imagine is staring at her? Is anyone staring at her?
2. *Pair work.*
   One person takes Kimberley's character, the other Lucy. Imagine a meeting between the two. Where does it take place? What is the outcome? Is it violent? Could their relationship develop over a period of time? Could they help each other?
3. Act out as a whole class or in small groups episodes outlining Kimberley's decline from stability.
4. Is it possible to take a more optimistic view? Could Kimberley return to stability? Could she leave the home and enter the outside world, even on a trial or temporary basis? What problems would she face? In small groups act out a scene in which Kimberley comes into contact with the outside world.

Ruby Edwards   *Page 44*

1. *For discussion*
   Why has Ruby turned to drink? Is her problem a common one? What will happen to Ruby in the future?
2. *Role-play*
   Place a volunteer, who will play Ruby, in the centre of the room. Arrange the class around her. The class speaks out the thoughts that are going through Ruby's mind (e.g. 'Will David come back?' 'What am I going to do?' 'Come on Ruby pull yourself together'). One half of the class could give negative thoughts whilst the rest are positive. Depending upon the strength of the thoughts presented, Ruby will respond accordingly.
3. Act out the following scenes:
   a) the day David left Ruby
   b) the day David returned.
4. *A final point*
   Who else could help Ruby?

Jackie   Page 44

1. *For discussion*
   Will Jackie see Gary again?
   Why does Jackie blame herself for the accident?
2. Design a poster warning people of the dangers of riding motor bikes dangerously. Make your design bold and eye-catching. Using the poster, invent a television commercial on the same theme. *Or* draw up a safety code for motorbike riders.
3. Act out the following scenes:
   a) Jackie meets Gary's mother in hospital
   b) Jackie meets a new boy and is asked to ride his motorbike.

Jimmy   Page 45

1. The group sits in a large circle. In turn, mime a famous celebrity or character. Continue the mime until the group has guessed who it is.
2. Following on from the game, name your hero or idol and explain what your admire about him/her.
3. Consider the character of Jimmy. Why does he think he's like James Dean?
4. In small groups, act out one of the following scenes:
   a) Jimmy at school
   b) Jimmy, 10 years later, still obsessed with his dead idol.
   c) a fan meeting his/her idol.

Shane   Page 45

1. Select two members of the group to take part in an observed improvisation with the group leader. The two members are friends who begin the scene sitting together on a street bench. The leader enters in role and accuses the friends of smashing a window in the next street.
   Observe the scene and try and decide if you are convinced about the friends' innocence.
2. Read the monologue 'Shane'. Consider his character and your immediate attitude towards him. Discuss this as a group, or in pairs. Build up a picture of his background, concentrating in particular on how he gets on with kids his own age.
3. In groups of three, role play a scene where the two friends witness one of Shane's acts of violence. This might be developed in further scenes with a larger group following up ideas from both this scene and the early one with the group leader.

4. Other scenes to develop on the theme of vandalism:
   a) the effect of vandalism on a small community
   b) a group of teenagers in a small town on a Saturday night
   c) a parent finding out that his/her child has been caught vandalising property.

Lynn	*Page 47*
Grandmother	*Page 48*
Ian	*Page 48*
Brenda	*Page 49*
Carol	*Page 49*

1. Try this game, called 'Break in'. The class stands in a circle with arms joined. The aim is to make the unit as strong as possible. The circle moves around. One class member who stands outside the circle tries to break into the centre. The circle tries to keep the person out. The circle can chant to help create strength e.g. 'Out – Out – Out' etc.

   If the room is too small for this activity try using two or three groups. These can go one at a time.

2. *Role-play*
   As an extension of this activity, act out a scene where a pupil in school tries to make friends in a group situation. E.g. a group of friends are in the classroom before the teacher arrives and they reject a new pupil. They might do this just by refusing to talk to him or her.)

3. Act out these scenes:
   a) Lynn entering her grandmother's house.
   b) Ian meeting Lynn.
   c) the scene at the disco.
   d) Brenda and Carol discuss the 'new girl', Lynn.
   e) Carol meets Lynn.

4. Using the monologues and these improvised scenes together you can build your own play about Lynn.

5. Write your own story about facing a new situation.